MASTERWORKS IN METAL

*A Millennium of Treasures
from the State Art Museum
of Georgia, USSR*

October 29, 1989 - January 7, 1990

MASTERWORKS

A Millennium of Treasures from the State Art

B Street Pier Exhibit Hall
San Diego, California

IN METAL
Museum of Georgia, USSR

An exhibition organized by
the Timken Art Gallery

Funding provided by
the San Diego
Unified Port District

This publication made
possible by a grant from
the Putnam Foundation

Published by
The Putnam Foundation
Timken Art Gallery
1500 El Prado, Balboa Park
San Diego, California 92101
Copyright © 1989 by The Put-
nam Foundation, Inc.
ISBN: 0-9610866-8-8
Cover: St. Mamai, Tondo of
Ghelati, 11th century (fig. 11)

Publication Coordinator/
Editor   Hal Fischer
Copy Editor   Judith Dunham
Design   Lilli Cristin Design,
Glendale
Typography   RS Typographics,
North Hollywood
Lithography   Typecraft, Inc.,
Pasadena
Photography   Ursula and
André Held

Masterworks in Metal:
A Millennium of Treasures
from the State Art Museum of
Georgia, USSR has been
organized in conjunction with
the 1989 San Diego Arts Festival:
Treasures of the Soviet Union.

Table of Contents

Foreword

WISDOM SUGGESTS that art is here to help us live.

The centuries-old religious art of Georgia has been brought to San Diego not only to help us live but to help us appreciate those who have lived before us.

These masterworks in gold and silver bring to mind the shared heritage of countries as different and distinct as the Soviet Union and the United States.

Just as we have reached across an ocean to discover these artifacts, the icons' creators have reached across a millennium to share them with us. We can only view them with deep respect, gratitude, and awe.

Similarly, it is with deep respect and gratitude that I thank those whose contemporary faith made this exhibit possible.

The earliest believers in the San Diego Arts Festival were Joan Kroc and Helen and David Copley. Without them, seeing these masterworks would have remained but a dream.

Next, I wish to thank the San Diego Unified Port District Commissioners, who underwrote the new permanent exhibit hall and the exhibit itself; the farsighted believers on the San Diego City Council; and John Lockwood, the resourceful City Manager.

It is to the Timken Art Gallery that I devote my most long-standing thanks. Since its doors opened, the Timken Art Gallery has permitted free access to all. In that traditional spirit of generosity, the Timken now brings MASTERWORKS IN METAL to San Diego with no profit to itself.

Inspired by the vision of the Putnam Foundation's early benefactors, Anne R. and Amy Putnam, the current trustees; Robert Ames, president; Nancy Ames Petersen, Director of the Timken Art Gallery; and Hal Fischer, project coordinator for this exhibit, have all helped to advance the Putnam sisters' hopes of shared experiences through art. Like the icons you will see, these people have contributed their own quiet blessing in order to bring this exhibit to San Diego.

The Soviets, too, contributed beyond mere measure. Valeri Asatiani, Minister of Culture for the Republic of Georgia, whose trust and faith permitted these rare and fragile objects to travel to the United States for the first time, deserves more than just our appreciation—as does Irina Mikheyeva, the Soviet Minister of Culture's chief representative for the entire arts festival.

Finally, a special thank you to the Ronald McDonald Children's Charities for providing the funding to admit children into the exhibit free.

Maureen O'Connor, Mayor
City of San Diego

Acknowledgments

IT IS A GREAT HONOR for the Timken Art Gallery to have been selected as the organizing institution for the first exhibition in the United States of medieval masterworks from the Soviet Socialist Republic of Georgia. We are deeply appreciative, and particularly indebted, to those individuals whose commitment has been central to the success of this project.

Dr. Tamaz Sanikidze, Director of the State Art Museum of Georgia, has given his full support and expertise to this effort. Eric Kartvelishvili and Marina Palavandishvili of the State Art Museum and Alex Graboviak of the Georgian Ministry of Education provided essential information and assistance.

An exhibition of this complexity requires the cooperation and talents of many people. MASTERWORKS IN METAL has been greatly enriched by the dedicated efforts of the following individuals: Dextra Frankel, exhibition designer; Jeffrey Cohen, graphic designer; Lilli Cristin, catalogue designer; and Vera Espinola, essayist and consultant scholar. Hal Fischer, exhibition coordinator, attended to every detail of this project, from loan negotiations and transport arrangements to staffing, education materials, and development of this catalogue. Lastly, the Directors of the Putnam Foundation join with me in extending our sincere gratitude to the people of Georgia. The loan of their most treasured patrimony—works of art that so eloquently communicate a noble history and a centuries-old religious devotion—exemplifies the generous and kind spirit of the Georgian people.

Nancy Ames Petersen, Director
Timken Art Gallery

Georgia

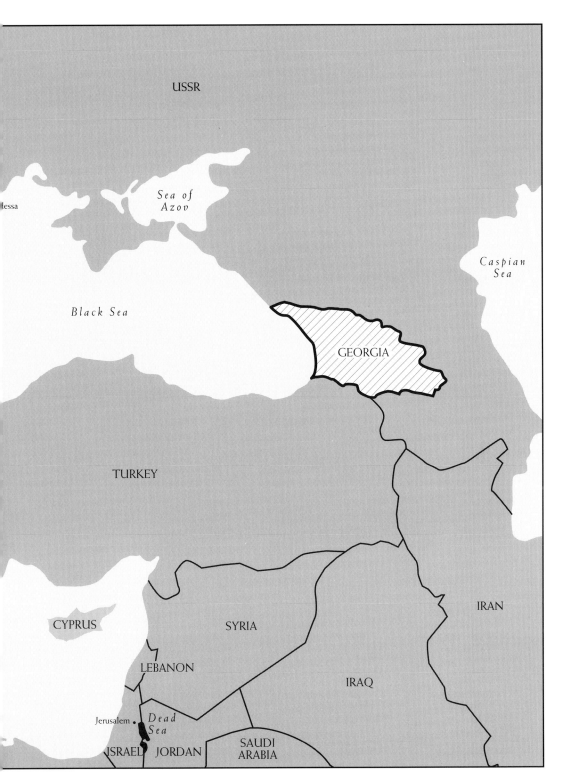

USSR

Sea of Azov

Caspian Sea

Black Sea

lessa

GEORGIA

TURKEY

IRAN

CYPRUS

SYRIA

LEBANON

IRAQ

Jerusalem • *Dead Sea*

SAUDI ARABIA

ISRAEL JORDAN

Georgia: Cities and Historical Sites

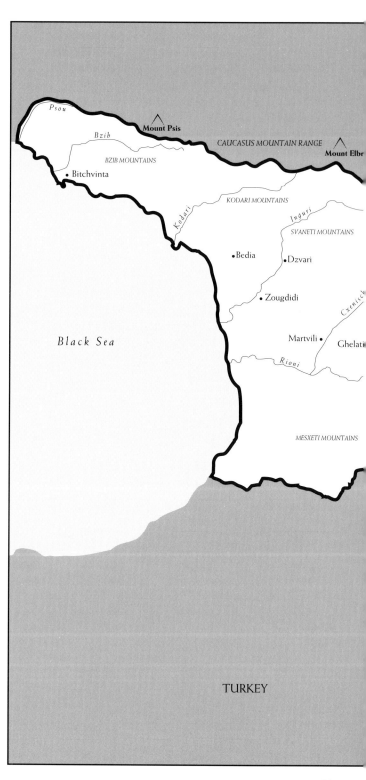

Psou

Mount Psis

Bzib

CAUCASUS MOUNTAIN RANGE

Mount Elbr

BZIB MOUNTAINS

• Bitchvinta

KODARI MOUNTAINS

Inguri

Kodari

SVANETI MOUNTAINS

•Bedia

•Dzvari

• Zougdidi

Cxenisc

Martvili •

Ghelati

Rioni

Black Sea

MESXETI MOUNTAINS

TURKEY

R

RUSSIAN SOVIET FEDERATED REPUBLIC

Tarak

CAUCASUS MOUNTAIN RANGE

Rioni

Mount Kazbek

• Nikorcminda

LOMI MOUNTAINS

Aragvi

G E O R G I A

KARTLI MOUNTAINS

CAUCASUS MOUNTAIN RANGE

• Alaverdi

Alazani

Kura

• Gori

Samtavisi •

Telavi •

GOMBORI MOUNTAINS

• Mtskheta

• Shouamta

TRIALETI MOUNTAINS

Tbilisi •

Trialeti •

Iori

• Pitareti

IORI PLATEAU

Kura

AZERBAIJAN

ARMENIA

IRAN

TRIPTYCH OF KHAKHOULI
Gold, gilded silver, precious and semiprecious stones, cloisonné enamel
12th century
57⅞ x 78¾ in. (147 x 200 cm.)

The Craft of the Georgian Gold- and Silversmiths

*F*ROM A BIRD'S-EYE VIEW, the Soviet Socialist Republic of Georgia is a sun-soaked corner of the earth. To the north are the majestic heights and eternal snows of the Caucasus mountain range; to the west, the coastline of the Black Sea, drowned in subtropical vegetation; farther away, to the south and east, the amazingly beautiful combination of fertile fields and rocky mountains.

The gold and silver work featured in MASTERWORKS IN METAL provides an idea of the general artistic and technical characteristics of this craft during the middle and late part of the Middle Ages. However, the culture of Georgia can be traced much further back in history. The oldest works of art found in this region—cave paintings, tools, and pottery—are thousands of years old. The heritage and longevity of Georgian civilization are evident today in countless monuments, historical sites, and works of art—ruins of colonies and ancient villages, majestic fortresses, temples adorned with paintings, sculptures, and gold and silver work.

Georgia is considered to be the oldest region in the world for the practice of metallurgy. In recent years archaeologists have discovered beautifully wrought gold ornaments dating from the end of the third millennium B.C. The artistic and technical quality of these treasures is proof of the Georgians' great skill in metalwork. Excavations have brought to light abundant archaeological material from the middle Bronze Age (the second millennium B.C.), a period of enormous economic and cultural progress for the Georgian tribes. Gold and silver objects, depicting rites and cults with great originality and delicately decorated with precious stones and filigree, were discovered in the excavations of the funerary mound at Trialeti in southeast Georgia. The evolution of local traditions, as well as certain features indicating the existence of links with the great cultures of the neighboring Near East, is evident in these works.

Between the second and first millennium B.C., two main regions developed: Colchis to the west and Iberia to the east. Each one had its own distinct culture, which is clearly reflected in its metalwork. The culture of Colchis is exemplified by bronze axes and openwork belt buckles elegantly designed and decorated with stylized animals, astral signs, and geometric figures. The bronze objects of Iberia display the same ornamental motifs; graphic signs are predominant, and the decoration recalls similar works of Aegean and Hittite art.

Social progress in Georgia was greatly encouraged by the discovery of iron and the subsequent development of iron smelting, which marked the end of the second millennium B.C. Ancient Greeks attribute the discovery of ways of working iron to the Georgian tribes, a fact supported by linguistic data and mythology. This important event in the history of mankind is central to the Greco-Georgian myth of Prometheus (Amiran in Georgian). Prometheus taught men to use fire and iron, thus provoking the anger of the gods, who chained him to rocks in the Caucasus. Historical evidence can be found in another myth as well: the expedition of the Argonauts, the quest for the Golden Fleece of the fabulously rich King Aites of Colchis (father of Medea).

Contact between Georgia and the Greek world rapidly increased at the beginning of the eighth century B.C., at which time Greek colonies appeared along the coast of the Black Sea in Colchis. Simultaneously, links with the Scythian and the Sarmatian cultures and Achaemenian Persia were strengthened. One of the most important commercial routes of the ancient world, the connection between the Black Sea and the Caspian Sea, passed through Georgia. This opened many possibilities for exchanges and contact between Georgia and neighboring countries. Thus cultural traditions of highly developed countries came to Georgian soil, where they influenced artistic life and were joined with local traditions.

In the seventh and sixth centuries B.C., new systems of government based on slavery emerged in Georgia. These entities subsequently collaborated and sometimes competed with countries of the Near East and the ancient world. This interaction aided the development of agriculture, craftsmanship, and commerce, and accelerated the ethnic consolidation of the Georgian tribes. Large villages appeared, and fortresses, palaces, temples, theaters, hippodromes, marketplaces, baths, and other edifices were built. According to Greek and Roman historians, and archaeological evidence, in Mtskheta, the capital of Iberia, a great number of noble edifices were erected for religious or civic purposes. This town became a prosperous commercial center and an important cultural center for the whole of Transcaucasia.

The high level of Georgian culture during antiquity is evident not only in architecture, but in other arts as well: sculpture, ceramics, glyptics, and especially metalwork. Archaeological excavations have brought to light artifacts from every region of the country. Most of the toreutics (embossed or chased work)[1] and jewelry of this period were created in local workshops and are original in form. The remainder, although made in Georgia, are replicas of the Greco-Roman or Achaemenian styles. Nevertheless, even objects that are clearly copies or imitations drawn from other cultures tend to evidence stylistic traits peculiar to Georgia.

Utilitarian and ritual objects in gold, silver, bronze, and iron from Akhalgori, Vani, Mtskheta, Satchkhera, and many other places are diverse in their decorative aspects. The Georgian artisans were skilled in a surprising range of techniques, including hammering, chasing, stamping, welding, granulation, and inlay. Polychromy (the art of combining many colors) and beading are characteristic of many toreutics of antiquity. Historical sources indicate that the technique of polychrome chasing was also known in Georgia. The production of copper and bronze statuettes was widespread, and a great number of these works have been preserved. Cloisonné work appeared in late antiquity, with the first examples dating to the second century B.C.

Thus, during antiquity a solid foundation—rooted in both ancient local traditions and technical progress—was developed by Georgian artists in the art of metalwork. It is from this firmly established tradition that the metalwork of medieval Georgia was to evolve.

With the establishment of Christianity in Georgia in A.D. 337, Georgian art entered a new phase. The history and culture of Georgia from the fourth through the eighteenth centuries A.D. were feudal. This span of time, nearly fourteen hundred years, can be divided into three major stages or historical eras: the early feudal period (fourth to tenth centuries); the middle or expansion period (tenth to fourteenth centuries); and the late period (fifteenth to eighteenth centuries).

In the development of Georgian art, the early feudal period is delineated by the creation of new themes and forms made in response to the Christian view of the world. This stage was marked by bitter struggle, first with Byzantium and Sassanian Persia, then with the Arabs, who conquered Georgia in the second half of the seventh century and held it for almost four hundred years.

At the beginning of the sixth century, Tbilisi became the capital of eastern Georgia and a significant cultural center. In different parts of the country, important buildings, extraordinary in their artistic and structural perfection, began to appear. These include the Basilica of Sion at Bolnissi (A.D. 478–493) and Djvari at Mtskheta (A.D. 587–604). Georgian monasteries were established in Syria and Palestine during this period, and later in Greece and Sinai. Very active in the field of literature and translation, these monasteries contributed enormously to the vast cultural exchange between Georgia and the surrounding countries.

The Arab invasion in the second half of the seventh century weakened and decentralized the country. In the late eighth and early ninth centuries, new forms of government appeared in southern, eastern, and western Georgia. Despite the influence of Islam, Georgian culture continued to develop its own artistic traditions with great vitality.

In stone and metalwork, flat graphic representation (partly linked to popular tradition) was well suited to an expression of a medieval vision of the world. Relief work on stone, embossing, and enameling of the eighth and ninth centuries were executed in this style. The RELIQUARY CROSS OF MARTVILI (fig. 1), with a scene of the Crucifixion on a background of niello, is an excellent example of this linear style. Noteworthy in this work from the monastery of Martvili in Samegrelo is the exaggerated emphasis on certain parts of the body (the head and hands), which intensifies the expressiveness of the representation.

By the second half of the tenth century, the beginning of the middle or expansion period, the linear style slowly gave way to a more volumetric depiction of forms in gold and silver. Political, economic, and cultural progress in Georgia during this time enabled metalwork to reach a stylistic high point. By the beginning of the eleventh century, the Arabs had been driven out of many provinces of Georgia. The country was united under the Bagrationi dynasty and soon was transformed into a strong feudal monarchy. At the time of King David IV (known as David the Builder, 1089–1125), an eminent statesman and warrior, and Queen Tamara (1184–1213),[2] legendary for her political statesmanship, Georgia became a powerful and centralized state. As a result, the Georgian empire, uniting all Transcaucasia and certain isolated parts of the Near East, grew more influential. Georgian statesmen took an active part in the life of Byzantium and the countries of the Christian East. Georgia became the stronghold of Orthodox Christianity in the Near East.

In the Georgian monasteries of Ghelati and Ikalto, academies were formed that contributed to the development of civilization. In the fields of literature and philosophy, ideas were born that bear comparison with those on which the Renaissance was based. At the end of the eleventh century, the great poet Sota Rustaveli wrote THE KNIGHT IN THE PANTHER'S SKIN, a masterpiece of world literature.

During the middle or expansion period, magnificent edifices were erected for civil or religious use. These include the cathedrals of Sveti-Tskhoveli in Mtskheta, Alaverdi in the province of Kakheth, and Bagrat in western Georgia. Striking examples of monumental fresco painting and mosaics from the Middle Ages still exist in many of the churches dating from this period.

As in previous periods, works of religious art, such as icons, altar and processional crosses, manuscript bindings, chalices, rhipidi, and other objects of ecclesiastical use, represent the apex of toreutics of the Middle Ages. These works, executed in gold or silver, richly decorated in a variety of ways (including mounted enamel work and precious stones), embody an artistic and technical perfection that has never been surpassed.

The development of gold and silver metalwork in the tenth and eleventh centuries was marked by one major concern: the problem of volumetric interpretation and plasticity. The PROCESSIONAL CROSS OF ISHKHANI (fig. 2), which carries an exact date of 973, is situated at a turning point. This work shows a tendency toward a plastic modeling of the human body, if only in the more general volumetric forms. The concerns of the preceding period are evident in the marked expressiveness of the face, hands, and legs. The CHALICE OF BEDIA (fig. 6) holds a place of importance among the gold and silver work of this period. The high relief, the almost natural proportions that the artist has managed to give the figures, and the free-flowing garments imbue this work with a sense of monumentality that belies its small scale. The extraordinarily realistic facial expressions add a certain liveliness of representation and afford a point of contrast.

An interest in Hellenistic traditions was revived during this period. At the same time, a style of expression emerged that was both national and individual in nature. The TONDO OF GHELATI (fig. 11) is a masterwork of Georgian medieval sculpture and is the work that, in a sense, completes the Georgian artisans' exploration of plastic form. The relief work on the tondo is practically in the round. The outline of the figures on the smooth background is strong and precise, and the forms are modeled with great skill. Certain parts of the drawing are interpreted in a decorative manner. The beautiful inscription on the upper part of the tondo lends to the sense of balance evident in this concise composition.

The beginning of the thirteenth century marked an end to the exploration of plasticity and volume by Georgian artists. New emphasis was placed on ornamental and decorative treatments of metallic surfaces. Metalwork from this period is distinguished by the use of brilliant materials, a luxury of decoration, an occasional overabundance of details, and a richness of precious stones and enamel mounting. Niello was once again widely used.

The large gold TRIPTYCH OF KHAKHOULI (pg.12), executed at the beginning of the twelfth century, blatantly manifests these new stylistic qualities. Ordered by Dimitrius I, son of David the Builder, the triptych surrounds a representation of the Mother of God, of whom only the face and the hands, rendered in cloisonné enamel, are preserved. The scroll ornament is distributed in a supple, ribbon-like fashion all around the immense gold surface. The entire triptych is luxuriously decorated with numerous medallions and plates, the oldest of which date from the eighth and ninth centuries, the most recent from the fifteenth century.[3] The great skill of execution and scale place this work among the masterpieces of the Middle Ages.

The majority of the cloisonné enamels that decorate the TRIPTYCH OF KHAKHOULI date from the twelfth century, the period in which this art enjoyed great popularity. From a technical perspective, these enamels are exquisite in their execution. The faces of the saints are expressive, the folds of the clothing complex, and the coloring subtle. The wine-colored tonality peculiar to Georgian enameling predominates. MASTERWORKS IN METAL includes several examples of cloisonné icons. PRESENTATION AT THE TEMPLE (fig. 15) is noteworthy for the Georgian church architecture that forms the background element of the composition.

The onset of the thirteenth century saw a decline in the political authority and independence of Georgia. In the middle of the century, Mongol hordes invaded. At the end of the fourteenth century, Timur's seven invasions resulted in the complete destruction of the country. By the late feudal period, Christian Georgia found itself surrounded by Islamic countries. It suffered devastating invasions from Turkey and Persia, and raids from northern Caucasian brigands. European states had neither the strength nor the interest to come to the rescue of a country that was no longer of political or economic interest. Thus Georgia turned to Russia, which was also Orthodox Christian. Bonds were created between the two countries, and in 1801 Georgia was attached to the Russian Empire.

This alliance signaled the dawn of a new era in the history of the Georgian people. The feudal foundations declined and capitalism was born. Georgian culture was joined with Russian culture, and through the latter rejoined the stream of European civilization.

Although the Middle Ages was a difficult time in the history of the Georgian people, artistic life during this epoch remained vital. In periods of relative calm and political and economic stability, Georgian architects, painters, miniaturists, and goldsmiths worked diligently, faithful to established traditions. At the same time, the art of Near Eastern cultures, particularly that of Persia, was influential.

From the eighteenth century on, the art of Georgian gold and silver metalwork maintained a sense of national identity. Yet Georgian art was subjected to considerable influences from Russia and western Europe, particularly in the area of iconography. At the end of the nineteenth century, mass-produced, stamped icons curtailed the evolution of the individually crafted icon.

The art of traditional metalworking was reintroduced in the 1950s, when, thanks to the very rich experience bequeathed by ancient Georgian masters, gold and silver work came to occupy a central position in Georgian Soviet art. The Soviet reality, the work, the daily life, the thoughts, and the feelings of our people—all these things inspire the famous Georgian goldsmiths, whose art has gained enormous popularity not only in the Soviet Union but in many countries throughout the world.

T. Sanikidze, Director
State Art Museum of Georgia, USSR

G. Abramishvili, Curator of the Treasury
State Art Museum of Georgia, USSR

NOTES

[1] Embossing, also known as repoussé, is the method of raising relief from the reverse side of a metal plate with hammers. Chasing, a finishing process, is the detailed working of raised metal surfaces with specialized tools from the front side of the plate. *Editor*

[2] In Georgia, the names of prominent female personages are often presented in masculine form. For example, Queen Tamara may also appear as Queen Tamar, or as King Tamar. Similarly, St. Nina, who is credited with converting Georgia to Christianity, is often referred to in the masculine form as St. Nino. *Editor*

[3] Icons were often modified over the centuries, e.g., additional plates or medallions could be added, or individual icons combined to form a larger work. *Editor*

Overleaf:
TRIPTYCH OF KHAKHOULI
Detail. Central top portion with cloisonné enamels of Christ,
St. John, and Apostles.

Georgian Ecclesiastical Objects

*T*HE NAME *Georgia* IS DERIVED from the Greek word for a culti-
vator of land, or farmer: *georgos, ge* meaning "earth," and *ergon,*
"work." The favorite artistic materials of the ancient Georgians,
stone and metal, came from the very earth they tilled. Converted to
Christianity by St. Nina (called Nino in Georgian) in A.D. 337, the
Georgian people used these gifts from the earth to interpret the
Christian message by constructing churches and monasteries of
stone and making icons and liturgical objects of metal. Georgian
ecclesiastical art thus became one of the oldest continuous traditions in Eastern Orthodoxy.

Stories about St. Nina, as well as numerous other saints and
legends associated with Christian Georgia, provided a fund for indig-
enous iconography. According to one story about St. Nina, she
was reputed to be a skilled doctor, and she went with the king and
the troops to subjugate and convert the pagans. Another version is
that St. Nina came to Georgia with twelve young women to start a
mission. The king was against her, but St. Nina cured his queen,
who was ill, and thereby performed her first miracle. St. Nina is said
to have died a martyr's death. While suffering, she asked for a cross,
but there was none. Given a grapevine, she fashioned a cross, but
the vine was not stiff, and so the cross arm sloped. This type of cross
still remains a symbol of Georgian Christianity.

Many other accounts are given about Christianity in Georgia.
One asserts that Georgia was considered the appanage of the Virgin
Mary, which may explain the Georgians' historical devotion to the
Mother of God, as she is known in Eastern Orthodoxy. According to
another story, St. Andrew brought Christianity to western Georgia
in the first century. St. George, the popular warrior saint, is often
called the patron saint of Georgia. Many of these legends, saints,
and Christian events were immortalized in ecclesiastical objects by
Georgian goldsmiths.

Although influenced by the Christian traditions of Byzantium
and Greece and by the invasions of non-Christian peoples such as
Arabs, Mongols, and Persians, medieval Georgia evolved an identifi-
able iconographic style unique unto itself. Many Georgian art historians describe the icon faces as "bold" or having "large, almond
eyes," and the flesh tones of the enamels as "wine-red." Also, Georgian design is regarded as less precise than the Byzantine, possessing
a "livelier look." We are told that Byzantine figures appear "out-

wardly calm, but with an inner tension," in contrast to the Georgian, which seem more emotional. These differences are attributed to religious attitudes and disparities in national character. In all the Georgian objects, be they metal, enamel, or painting, the "genetic eye" of the artist captures its own face, traditional forms,and collective history, intertwining them with the stylistic roots of Orthodox Christianity.

Eastern Orthodox liturgical objects had definite forms and specific uses dictated by church canon. The basic tenets of Eastern Orthodoxy governed its Christian symbols, occasionally adding or subtracting symbols to allow for cultural traditions within the confines of Orthodox Christian thought.

Metalwork and cloisonné enamels formed the mainstream of Georgian ecclesiastical art. Medieval Georgian metal icons were unique within Eastern Orthodoxy. They were often constructed by repoussé, chasing, or engraving of solid sheets of silver or gold and decorated with gilt, niello, precious stones, and pearls. These metal objects were made as complete icons, not simply as metal covers over painted wooden panels, as was often found on Russian and other Eastern Orthodox icons.

An Eastern Orthodox icon is an image of a sacred person or persons (such as Jesus Christ, the Mother of God, or a saint), or sacred events or feasts of the church year (such as the Nativity of Jesus Christ or the Annunciation), which has been blessed by a priest for holy use. The intent of the creation transcends its material worth. Even a humble sketch on paper is considered an icon if it has been consecrated to God. Icons are incensed during the liturgy, blessed with holy water, kissed, touched, and used for prayer and contemplation. They have candles burned before them, are used in ecclesiastical processions, and are given as memorials and gifts. Some icons are even said to be miraculous.

The form, size, and composition of an Orthodox icon vary. The most familiar icon is often a rectangular wooden panel, averaging about thirty centimeters in height and painted with pigments in an egg tempera medium over gesso. Infrequent opportunities to see other types of icons, such as the Georgian masterpieces handmade of precious metals featured in this exhibition, have contributed to an erroneous impression that all icons are painted. Icons have been carved in wood, ivory, and stone; made of cast copper alloys, champlevé and cloisonné polychrome enamels, ceramics, and mosaics; and made of textiles embroidered with threads of cotton, silk, gold, or silver. They have also been created of reverse paintings on glass or paintings on canvas or wood adorned with metals and precious or paste gems. Today, many Orthodox churches and homes, sometimes unable to obtain handcrafted icons, have icons simply made of paper pictures pasted on wood.

Icons from an altar screen *(iconostasis)* are often painted on gesso over a wooden support and may reach human height, whereas others, composed of any variety of materials, may even be small enough to fit into the palm of one's hand. Icons were also created in varied shapes. Archaeological excavations have yielded small, round, medallionlike metal icons. Rectangular, square, round, and oval icons have been constructed of wood, paint, metal, stone, mosaic, enamel, or ceramic. Single-panel icons of any shape, but mostly made of metals or enamels, are sometimes described as plaque icons. Diptych, triptych, and "quadriptych" icons containing, respectively, two, three, or four hinged sections were often made of cast metal, but some were also made of painted or carved wooden panels or sections of composite materials.

St. George, Icon of Tsvirli-Tchobeni (fig. 7), circa tenth and eleventh centuries, is an example of a typical Georgian medieval icon in its shape, construction, and iconography. It is an average size, twenty-nine by twenty-four centimeters, and was made by repoussé and chasing on silver. The subject is identified according to Orthodox tradition, by Old Georgian uncials. Eastern Orthodox icons, almost without exception, have identifying inscriptions either in Greek or in the liturgical language of the originating country.

Georgian metal icons were often made of one sheet of silver or gold by the repoussé technique, which means a high or low relief raised by hammering on the reverse side of the metal. The metal sheet was placed face down on a block of pitch. Each goldsmith or silversmith mixed his own pitch according to carefully guarded secret recipes that often included wax, sand, or ocher in a resin base. The pitch had to be slightly adhesive—to steady the metal against the blows of the hammer—and it also had to be yielding—to accommodate the various depths made in the metal. The smith used many hammers of various sizes to create the reversed design, carefully heating the metal in the block of pitch as the work progressed in order to eliminate metal stress and accompanying tears.

When the design was completed, the metal was heated to release it from the block, and pitch was added to the hollows of the relief as reinforcement for the finishing process, called chasing. For this procedure, the sheet was turned face up, and the outlines of the repoussé work were sharpened and delineated with a series of specialized chasing tools and hammers. Another technique on the face, or recto, was engraving, a process whereby metal was incised to form curved or straight lines of varying widths. The smith may have had several hundred small tools—with a few favorites among them—which he used to achieve the special effects needed in his work.

Pure silver and gold were often alloyed with less noble metals to achieve greater resistance, durability, and variety of color. When the metalworking was completed, silver objects were often partially or completely gilded by the mercury amalgam method. Mercury was mixed with gold and spread over the object, sometimes using a piece of cork. The mercury was then driven off by slow heating until only the gold remained. When gilding is no longer visible on an ancient object but is suspected to have once existed, X-ray fluorescence spectroscopy can still detect the surface presence of mercury long after the gold has worn away. Since the mid-nineteenth century, the toxic mercury method has been replaced by electroplating.

Niello, also used to decorate some medieval Georgian ecclesiastical objects, is a technique that produces black surfaces on gold, silver, or other, lighter backgrounds. This is often achieved by the heated fusing of silver sulphide onto a prepared area. Ancient niellos were frequently composed of silver, but other metals were also used, according to eleventh-century accounts of the monk Theophilus. The finished product was then burnished.

The oldest object in this exhibit is the ninth-century quatrefoil silver RELIQUARY CROSS OF MARTVILI (fig. 1). This exquisite medieval Georgian niello work renders a powerful simplicity to the linear figure of Christ crucified. The hinges at the top and the base (as seen from the back of the cross) indicate where it opened for the keeping of relics. The chain indicates that this was a pectoral cross, possibly worn by a bishop.

ST. NICHOLAS and ST. BASIL (figs. 9, 10), made in 1040 by master Ivan Monisdze, are excellent examples of Georgian gilded-silver plaque icons. Made by repoussé and chasing, these plates are inscribed in Old Georgian with details of the donor, the date, and the name of the goldsmith. They were probably part of a larger ecclesiastical work.

The TONDO OF GHELATI (fig. 11), a partially gilded disk twenty centimeters in diameter and dating from the eleventh century, is a unique work in repoussé whose figures are in such high relief that they are almost three-dimensional sculpture. For this most difficult technique, care must be taken to keep the thickness of the metal uniform while adjusting the heights of different areas to create correct proportions. The inscriptions had to be reversed on the back if they were to read from the front. Individual letters would appear taller and wider than the inscribed sketch and look crowded in the repoussé process unless they were made thinner and shorter. Georgian ecclesiastical art never moved beyond the form of high relief as did Western art, due to an Orthodox ban on the use of statues and images in sculptural form.

Most of the icons in this exhibit have Georgian geographical place names that often indicate monasteries or churches to which the icons were donated. Such is the ICON OF MARTVILI (fig. 3), dated tenth century, representing a standing figure of the Mother of God. With her right hand, she points to the figure of the Christ Child. This full-length view is one variant of the Hodigitria, a Greek title of unknown origin. A formal pose, the Hodigitria typically shows the Child Immanuel, rather than a baby, seated on his mother's left arm. The right hand of the Mother of God points to her son, whose face imparts a sense of wisdom, as The Way.

Eastern Orthodoxy has more than five hundred different types of iconographic styles depicting the Mother of God. Another of the standing Hodigitria type can be seen in the sixteenth-century ICON OF BITCHVINTA (fig. 21), made by repoussé and chasing on silver with gilt, turquoise, sapphires, and rubies. This fairly large icon, measuring almost forty centimeters tall, was also a reliquary used to house the remains of sacred objects or saints in a special area on the reverse. An even larger icon (sixty centimeters tall), the sixteenth-century TRIPTYCH OF ALAVERDI (fig. 23), was made by repoussé on silver with gilt and semiprecious stones. The central panel also depicts the Mother of God in the Hodigitria standing posture.

Only one Hodigitria icon in this exhibition does not show the Mother and Child in full length. It is the sixteenth-century ICON OF THE VIRGIN AND CHILD OF AKHALI-SHOUAMTA (fig. 22) with faces painted on wood. It was made by repoussé and chasing on silver and is adorned with gilt and semiprecious stones. The structure of this icon appears similar to Russian icons with metal *oklads* (icon covers), although the Georgian tradition is maintained by depicting the hands and feet in metal. In the eighteenth century, Russian icons with this type of Hodigitria iconography began to be known as the "Georgian Mother of God," probably due to Russia's increased contacts with its Christian neighbor to the south.

Icons of the sixteenth and seventeenth centuries often reveal foreign influences, especially from Persia. THE SAVIOUR, ICON OF NESPERI (fig. 24), from the sixteenth century, shows such qualities in the elaborately chased and engraved leaf and vine background and in the use of turquoise.

The sixteenth-century JOHN THE BAPTIST, ICON OF TELAVI (fig. 20) and the nineteenth-century ST. GEORGE, ICON OF ZOUGDIDI (fig. 30) each demonstrate traditional Georgian work in the central panel, however elaborate floral designs on the borders reflect Persian influences. The designs on the ICON OF TELAVI were made by engraving and chasing; those on the ICON OF ZOUGDIDI, by repoussé and chasing.

The manufacture of glass and vitreous substances in the Mtskheta area of Georgia was an unbroken tradition since pre-Christian times. Both the cloisonné and champlevé techniques were known, but all of the enamels in this exhibit were executed by the cloisonné method on gold.

Enamels adhere best to gold. The areas of the metal to be enameled were roughened for better adhesion and divided by thin gold wires into compartments or *cloisons*. Sometimes the *cloisons* were soldered to the back plate, but sometimes only the peripheral *cloisons* were soldered and the others were affixed by a paste or gum such as tragacanth. When filled with the vitreous frit and fired, the *cloisons* were firmly fused into place. Absolute cleanliness was essential in making enamels, or they did not hold well, resulting in a defective product.

Colored glass for making enamels was ground in a mortar and pestle. The coarser the grind, the more brilliant the colors. But if too coarse, the enamels would not fill the spaces and retained air bubbles when fired, which adversely affected the durability of the finished work. Usually, the enamels were fired several times. The process was extremely delicate and had to be watched constantly. At any stage, the enamels could crack or chip if the proper technique was not observed. When finished, the enamel surfaces were uneven and had to be ground and polished.

The twelfth and thirteenth centuries were a highly significant period in Georgian enameling. The thirteenth century is said to signify the end of enameling in Georgia due to the decline of Byzantium and also due to internal unrest and the invasion of the Mongols. As the economy declined, the production of luxury items diminished, including enamels and repoussé work, both of which were dependent on gold.

The twelfth-century cloisonné medallions of Christ and St. Demetrius (fig. 17, 18) are among the finest Georgian enamels in this exhibition. They once adorned the icon of the archangel Michael in the monastery of Djoumati. The inscriptions are in Old Georgian. Christ raises his right hand in a traditional benediction. The enamel colors remain bright and strong, equalling the intensity of the figures.

Although icons and processional crosses were incorporated into the liturgy of the Eastern Orthodox Church at different times and occasions, the chalices and rhipidi, or sacramental fans, had significant roles in the celebration of the Eucharist.

The tenth-century CHALICE OF BEDIA (fig. 6), made to hold the Communion wine, once stood on a pedestal base, which is now lost. The wine is consecrated as the Blood of Christ during the liturgy. The accompanying bread is consecrated as the Body of Christ. Rhipidi were used to fan insects away from these holy gifts during pontifical services at which the bishop presided. The CHALICE OF BEDIA is a masterpiece of workmanship, constructed of a single sheet of ducat gold by repoussé and chasing.

The exhibited icons and ecclesiastical objects of Georgia are not only masterworks in metal, but representations of ten centuries of creativity and spirituality. The people they once served are now silent, but their objects live on as a testimony to their ingenuity and faith. Perhaps this integrity of spirit is the greatest of all the masterworks.

Vera Beaver-Bricken Espinola

SELECTED BIBLIOGRAPHY

Abramaishvili, G., and T. Sanikidzé. *Orfèvrerie géorgienne du VIIe au XIXe siècle*. Geneva: Musée d'Art et d'Histoire, 1979.

Alibegasvil, G., and A. Volkskaja. "The Icons of Georgia." *The Icon*. New York: Alfred A. Knopf, 1982.

Antonova, V. I., and N. E. Mneva. *Katalog Drevnerusskoi Zhivopis'*. Vol. I and II. Moscow: Isskusstvo, 1963.

Belen'kaya, D. A. "Kresti i Ikonki iz Kurganov Podmoscovya." *Sovietskaya Arkhiologia* 4 (1976).

Beridze, Vaxtang, et al. *The Treasures of Georgia*. Trans. Bruce Penman. London: Century Publishing, 1984.

Hapgood, Isabel Florence. *Service Book of the Holy Orthodox-Catholic Church*. 5th ed. Englewood, N.J.: Antiochian Orthodox Christian Archdiocese, 1975.

Hopko, Fr. Thomas. *Worship: The Orthodox Faith*. Vol. II. 2nd ed. New York: The Department of Religious Education, The Orthodox Church in America, 1976.

Maryon, Herbert. *Metalwork and Enamelling*. 5th ed. New York: Dover Publications, 1971.

Mepisashvili, Rusudan, and Vakhtang Tsintsadze. *The Arts of Ancient Georgia*. U.S.A.: Thames and Hudson Inc., 1979.

Ware, Archimandrite Kallistos. *The Orthodox Way*. Crestwood, N.Y.: St. Vladimir's Orthodox Theological Seminary, 1979.

Catalogue of the Exhibition

Vera Beaver-Bricken Espinola   *VBE*
Tina Popkhadze Sarran   *TPS*

1   RELIQUARY CROSS OF
MARTVILI
Gilded silver, niello
9th century
6⅞ x 3½ x 2 in. (15 x 9 x 5 cm.)

The RELIQUARY CROSS OF MART-
VILI depicts the Crucifixion.
On either side of Christ are the
figures of the Mother of God and
St. John the Evangelist. The flat,
linear style of representation,
which gives this work its sense
of powerful simplicity, is characteristic of ninth-century Georgian art. The exaggerated head
and hands of the Christ figure add
to the expressiveness of the work.

The cross belonged to the
monastery of Martvili, in Samegrelo, a historic province of Georgia. Old Georgian inscriptions on
the reverse state the names of
Queen Khosrovanouch, wife of
south Georgian eristavi Sumbat I
Mapal (died 889), and her two
sons, Bagrat and David. *TPS*

The hinges at the top and
base, as seen from the back of the
cross, indicate where it opened
for the keeping of relics. The
chain suggests that this was a
pectoral cross, possibly worn by
a bishop. *VBE*

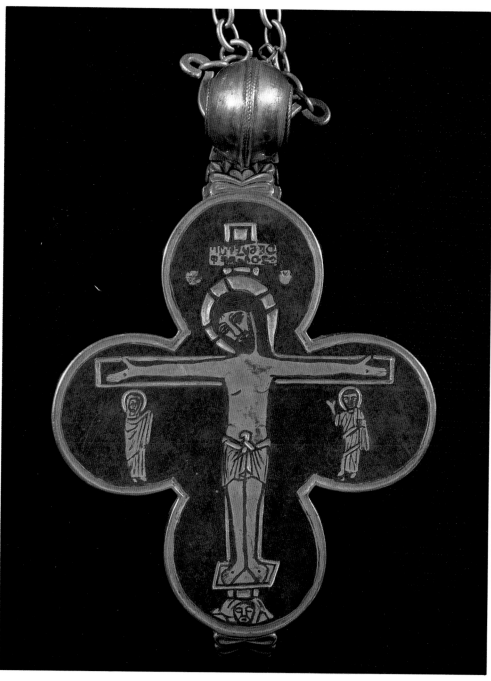

2   PROCESSIONAL CROSS OF
    ISHKHANI
    Gilded silver
    973
    8⅝ x 5⅞ in. (22 x 15 cm.)

Only a few fragments of the cross
remain: the center part with
crucifix, the handle, and several
ornamental medallions. The rendering of the Christ figure is ex-
emplary of the Georgian artists'
growing interest in more
volumetric or sculptural representations of the human form. In
depicting Christ's suffering, the
artist has modelled the figure to
give particular attention to both
proportion and detail.

    The inscription on the cross
mentions the exact date and the
name of the donor. The cross was
given to the church of Ishkhani
in Tao-Klardjetie, a historic region in southern Georgia, by the
Bishop Illarion. *TPS*

31

3   ICON OF MARTVILI
    Gold, gilded silver, cloisonné
    enamel, pearls, turquoises,
    semiprecious stones
    10th century
    12⅝ x 9 x ⅝ in.
    (32 x 23 x 1.5 cm.)

The central portion of this icon,
which was made by repoussé and
chasing on gold, is adorned with
pearls, semiprecious stones,
and round enamel plaques with
images of Jesus Christ and the
Mother of God. The central portion is secured to the gilded silver outer frame with small nails.
The outer frame features six
large and three small round
enamel plaques with the images
of saints. All of the enamel
plaques have inscriptions, but
the main central panel, depicting
the Mother of God, does not.
VBE

 The central panel of the ICON
OF MARTVILI shows the Mother
of God in a standing, full-length
Hodigitria pose. Certain aspects
of this panel are especially typical
of Georgia, such as the use of the
grape leaf decoration and the
inclusion of sardoliques (stones
from the Caucasus Mountains).
TPS

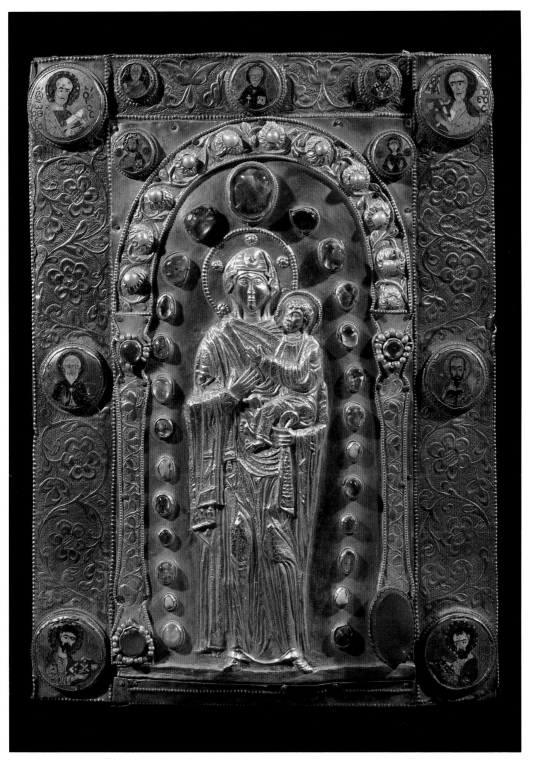

4　PLATE OF SAGOLASHENI:
　THE ANNUNCIATION
　Silver, partially gilded
　10th–11th century
　13⅝ x 12 in. (34.5 x 30.5 cm.)

This is one of a set of twelve plates depicting scenes from the life of Christ. There are only five surviving plates; the other remaining plates are THE VISITATION, THE PRESENTATION AT THE TEMPLE, THE ASCENSION, and THE BAPTISM. Each plate bears a number indicating its order of presentation. The function of the plates is unknown, but one hypothesis is that they were used as decoration on the chancel.

THE ANNUNCIATION, the plate pictured here, has a traditional decorative Georgian grape leaf motif. The use of grape leaf ornamentation in this and other centuries-old works is but one indication that wine making has been a prominent part of Georgian life for hundreds of years. *TPS*

The iconography of this work places it in the category of an icon, but its use as such is said to be unconfirmed. The lack of inscriptions is exceptional for an Eastern Orthodox ecclesiastical object. *VBE*

5   PROCESSIONAL CROSS
     OF BRETI
     Master Gabriel Safareli
     Gilded silver
     994–1001
     33⅞ x 20 in. (86 x 51 cm.)

All processional crosses have depictions of the Crucifixion. The PROCESSIONAL CROSS OF BRETI also includes images of the Mother of God and St. John in the ends of the left and right arms; images of the Evangelists and archangels appear on the highly decorated handle. The figures of the saints were executed separately and soldered later onto the surface of the cross.

Engravings and inscriptions on the cross give the names of the artist, the donors, and historical personages. Whereas some Georgian crosses carry the names of their makers, it is more common to find the name of the donor, as opposed to the artist, because in earlier times artists felt it was sinful to put their names near the image of God. The inscription on this cross mentions King Bagrat III (975–1014) and Michael, Father Superior of Safar Monastery. *TPS*

The bottom of the cross was shortened at one time, as can be seen by the reinforcements near Christ's knees and the nearby misaligned borders. The figure of Christ, however, is intact and does not show a break where the cross was fractured. Because the figure is whole, it could have been a separate object that was not affixed to the cross when it was damaged. Further technical studies may yield more information about this fascinating piece.

The depiction of Christ on this cross is unusual in Eastern Orthodoxy because the two feet are nailed one on top of the other, with one nail, as in Western crucifixes. Orthodox crucifixes usually show a nail driven separately through each foot, as in the PROCESSIONAL CROSS OF ISHKHANI (fig. 2). *VBE*

6   CHALICE OF BEDIA
     Ducat gold
     999
     5½ x 5½ in. (14 x 14 cm.)

The exterior surface of this masterpiece shows twelve figures, each in a compartment defined by colonnades reminiscent of the stone altar screens in early Georgian churches. Seated figures of Christ Pantocrator and the Hodigitria Mother of God and Christ Child occupy two of the sections. The other ten depict the standing figures of saints John, Andrew, Luke, Mark, Paul, Peter, Lebbeus, Thomas, Bartholomew, and James. Old Georgian inscriptions identify the saints and give the names of the donors, King Bagrat III and his mother, Queen Gourandoukhth, dating the chalice to 999. *VBE*

King Bagrat III, ruler of the Abkhazes and the Kartvels, was responsible for the unification of Georgia in the late tenth to early eleventh centuries. He and his mother requested that the monastery of Bedia be constructed and the chalice be crafted for ceremonial use. The chalice, constructed of a single sheet of ducat gold, was made to hold the Communion wine. It originally stood on a gold pedestal base, which was lost. A later, silver pedestal base disappeared at the beginning of the twentieth century. The high relief, natural proportions, and expressive faces make this a masterpiece of Georgian metalwork. *TPS*

7   ST. GEORGE, ICON OF
    TSVIRLI-TCHOBENI
    Silver
    10th–11th century
    11⅜ x 9½ in. (29 x 24 cm.)

St. George is seen on horseback killing Roman emperor Diocletian, persecutor of Christians. This uniquely Georgian theme reflected political pressures from Byzantium in the last decades of the tenth century. Representations of St. George were quite rare in Byzantium and Eastern Orthodox countries prior to the twelfth century. *VBE*

St. George is considered the patron saint of Georgia. His popularity is reflected in the number of churches carrying his name and the fact that in some regions of the country he was sometimes venerated more than Christ. St. George lived in Cappadocia, a small country near Byzantium, in the third century. After receiving Christianity, he was tortured and killed by Diocletian, and subsequently resurrected. The apocryphal scene depicted here can be interpreted as the triumph of Christianity over paganism.

The inscriptions that appear on Eastern Orthodox icons denote their spiritual intentions or purpose, or serve as identification. The Old Georgian inscription on this icon mentions St. George. Portraits of warrior saints appear in each corner of the icon. The ICON OF TSVIRLI-TCHOBENI is from Svanetia, a mountainous region of Georgia. *TPS*

8   Rhipid of Zarzma
     Silver
     10th–11th century
     23¼ x 17⅞ in. (59 x 45.5 cm.)

One side of this quatrefoil form depicts a procession of angels carrying rhipidi and the Eucharistic gifts of bread and wine. The other side features a six-winged seraphim, the highest of the nine orders of angels. Alongside this celestial being are the signs of the four Evangelists (Matthew, Mark, Luke, and John), symbolized by man (the hands), lion, ox, and eagle. In the liturgy followed today, the rhipid is often carried in processions. In earlier times rhipidi, or sacramental fans, were used to fan insects away from the holy gifts (bread and wine) during pontifical services at which the bishop presided. *VBE*

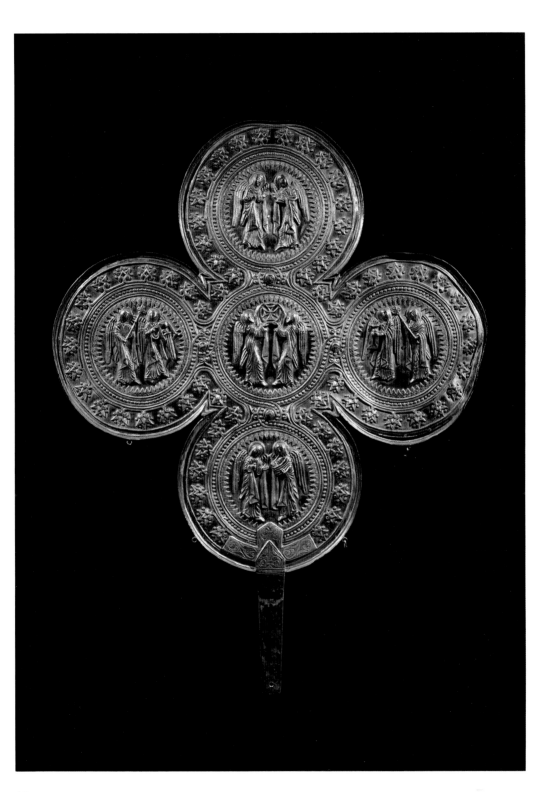

9   ST. NICHOLAS
    Master Ivan Monisdze
    Gilded silver
    1040
    7⅛ x 3 in. (18 x 7.5 cm.)

10 ST. BASIL
    Master Ivan Monisdze
    Gilded silver
    1040
    7⅛ x 3 in. (18 x 7.5 cm.)

These two plates are noteworthy
for their skillful modeling, which
communicates volumetric
representation. This is especially
evident in the rendering of the
clothing, in which the carefully
delineated folds provide clear outlines of the body while creating
a decorative linear motif. Each
saint is shown holding the gospel
and St. Nicholas is depicted
with his right hand raised for
the blessing.

Old Georgian inscriptions
mention the name of the donor,
Eudemon, patriarch of the monastery of Chemochmedi, and also
that of master craftsman Ivan
Monisdze. In addition to this
long inscription, another nota-
tion near St. Nicholas's foot
gives the exact date—1040.
These pieces were most likely
part of a larger ecclesiastical
object. *TPS*

11 St. Mamai,
   Tondo of Ghelati
   Silver, partially gilded
   11th century
   7⅞ x 7⅞ in. (20 x 20 cm.)

The function of the tondo is unknown, but it may have been part
of a banner carried in processions
or served as decoration on the
chancel. St. Mamai, who lived in
Caesarea, adopted Christianity in
the third century. He was thrown
to the lions, who did not harm
him, but was then speared to
death by Roman soldiers. In Byzantine art he is shown as a young
man being killed—a victim.
In Georgian art he is depicted as
a victor over death, holding the
sign of martyrdom, a cross, and
riding in triumph on the back
of a fierce lion. *VBE*

     In the Georgian language the
word *mamai* means father; thus
St. Mamai translates to St. Father,
which is the inscription that
appears on this plate. According
to the stories of Basil the Great and
Gregory of Nazianza, St. Mamai
was tortured on 2 September 275.

     The Tondo of Ghelati
represents the apex of Georgian
relief work—what might be
considered the last step before
three-dimensional representation.
Although sculpture in the round
was acceptable and even characteristic of representation within
the Roman Catholic church, this
technique was prohibited within
Eastern Orthodoxy.

The actual date of this work
is uncertain. While the style is
considered typical of the eleventh
century, some specialists date
it to the sixth century, based on
the fact that artists of the early
Christian era worked in high
relief, and partial gilding was
characteristic of that period. The
tondo is from the monastery of
Ghelati, which was built in 1106
by King David IV, who is credited
with making Georgia into a powerful and centralized nation. *TPS*

47

12   RELIQUARY CROSS OF
     MARTVILI
     Gold, cloisonné enamel,
     emeralds, rubies, turquoises,
     pearls
     10th century
     5⅞ x 3½ x 1⅛ in.
     (15 x 9 x 3 cm.)

This tenth-century reliquary cross carries inscriptions in Greek and Old Georgian. Hinges indicate where it opens to receive relics. The gold crucifix has a profusion of decorative elements: precious and semiprecious stones, pearls, and cloisonné enamel. The size of this cross is comparable with that of the ninth-century reliquary cross (fig. 1), and for this reason it may also have been used by a bishop. *VBE*

One side of the cross shows the figure of Christ on the cross, with the Mother of God to his right, St. John to his left, and the archangels Michael and Gabriel above and below. The reverse shows the Mother of God holding the Christ Child, and the four Evangelists, one in each arm of the cross. *TPS*

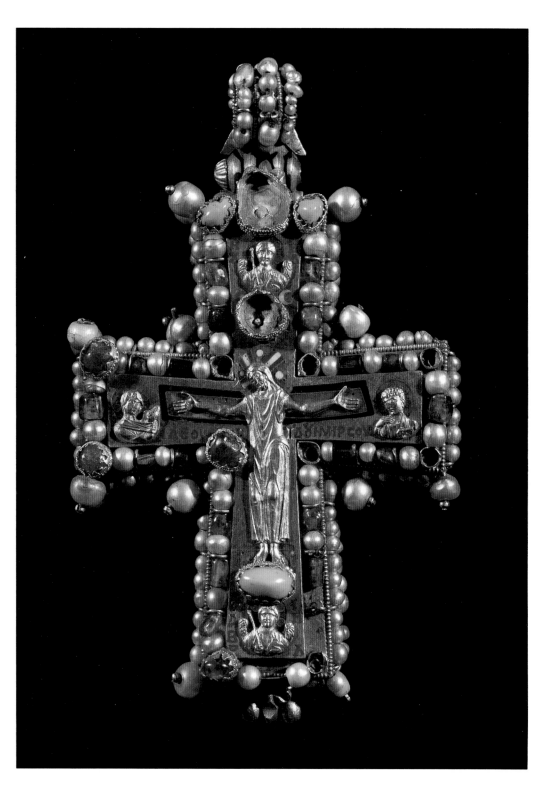

49

13 PANAGIA OF MARTVILI
Gold, silver, cloisonné
enamel, pearls
10th century
3⅛ x 2⅛ in. (8 x 5.5 cm.)

Although this piece is described
in its title as a *panagia*, the
hinges indicate that it is in fact a
reliquary. *Panagia* (Greek meaning "all holy") generally refers to
a small, circular holy image of the
Mother of God and the Christ
Child and is worn by a bishop
on his breast.

This reliquary has the same
quatrefoil shape found on the
ninth-century RELIQUARY CROSS
OF MARTVILI (fig. 1). It is made of
polychrome cloisonné enamel
outlined with pearls. The Greek
inscription stands for *Anastasis*,
meaning "The Resurrection."
This is known as the Paschal, or
Easter, icon, and shows Christ
freeing Adam and Eve, who sym-
bolize all men and women, by
trampling down the gates of
Hades and saving the captives
from death. It is the image of the
victor destroying death and offering eternal life. *VBE*

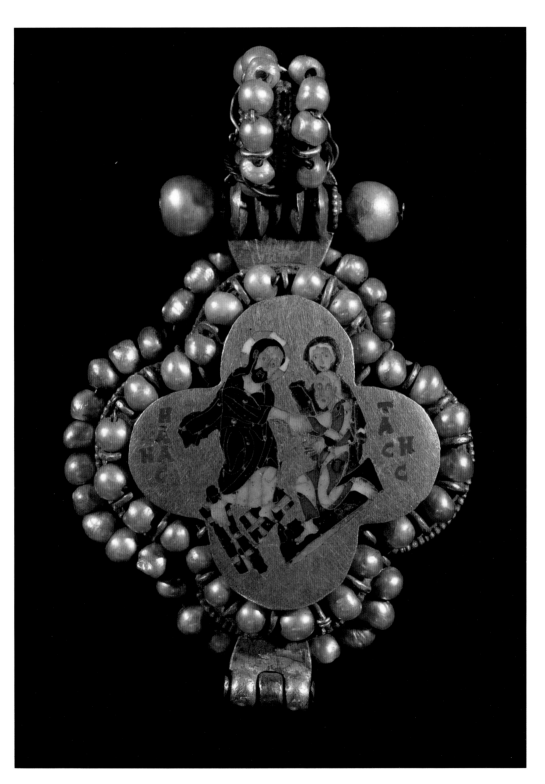

14 RELIQUARY
    Gold, silver, cloisonné
    enamel
    11th century
    3⅛ x 2⅜ in. (8 x 6 cm.)

This eleventh-century reliquary,
oval and hinged on the side,
shows Christ crucified on Gol-
gotha, the hill where crucifix-
ions took place, known as the
"skull place" and also as Calvary.
The skull of Adam is symboli-
cally depicted at the feet of
Christ. Angels watch over him
while Mary and St. John keep a
vigil at the cross. *VBE*

     This reliquary carries in-
scriptions in Old Georgian and
Greek. Christ is represented in a
colobian, a clothed depiction
more characteristic of earlier
iconographic treatments. The
use of many colors and a lively
expression are typical of Georgian art of this period. *TPS*

53

15 PRESENTATION
    AT THE TEMPLE
    Gold, cloisonné enamel
    12th century
    4¾ x 3⅞ in. (12 x 10 cm.)

This polychrome cloisonné enamel icon represents the Presentation at the Temple, one of the twelve major feasts of the church year, celebrated on 2 February according to the new (Gregorian) calendar and thirteen days later according to the old (Julian) calendar. Forty days after Christ was born, his parents brought him to the Temple of Jerusalem. According to Mosaic law, if a woman's first child is a boy, he shall be dedicated to the Lord. The meeting of Christ by the elder Simeon and the prophetess Anna is described in Luke 2:22–36:

At the time Jesus' parents also offered their sacrifice for purification—either a pair of turtledoves or two young pigeons was the legal requirement. That day a man named Simeon, a Jerusalem resident, was in the Temple. He was a good man, very devout, filled with the Holy Spirit and constantly expecting the Messiah to come soon. For the Holy Spirit had revealed to him that he would not die until he had seen him—God's anointed King. The Holy Spirit had compelled him to go to the Temple that day; and so when Mary and Joseph had arrived to present the baby Jesus to the Lord in obedience to the law, Simeon was there and took the child in his arms, praising God.

"Lord," he said, "now I shall die content! For I have seen him as you promised me. I have seen the Saviour you have given to the world. He is the light that will shine upon nations, and he will be the glory of your people, Israel." (THE BOOK, Tyndale Publishers, 8th ed.)

The celebration of this feast day in the church symbolizes the meeting of the Messiah by the congregation, who can claim their own meeting with the Lord and can "depart in peace" since their eyes have seen the salvation of God in the presence of his Christ (Anointed One). It is customary in many churches to bless candles on the feast of the Meeting of the Lord. When or where this custom originated is not known. Some Georgian art historians say that candles were not shown in Byzantine iconographic representations of this feast day, but have been used in Georgian and Western church art. An unusual feature of this icon is the lack of inscriptions. *VBE*

As evidenced by the holes around the edges, this small icon was possibly part of a larger piece. PRESENTATION AT THE TEMPLE is thought to be part of a set, of which the only other known remaining works are the RESURRECTION OF LAZARUS (fig. 16) and the DESCENT OF THE HOLY SPIRIT. Of particular interest is the attention the artist has given to the traditional Georgian church architecture that forms a beautiful background for the central figures. *TPS*

16 RESURRECTION OF LAZARUS
    Gold, cloisonné enamel
    12th century
    4⅞ x 3⅞ in. (12.5 x 10 cm.)

The feast of the Resurrection of
Lazarus is celebrated the
Saturday before the entrance of
Christ into Jerusalem (Palm Sun-
day). Although not one of the
twelve major feasts of the church
year, it falls into the group of feasts
celebrated during the Lenten sea-
son. The date is dependent upon
the date of Easter, which in the
Eastern Orthodox church is cal-
culated according to the spring
equinox and never occurs before
the Jewish Passover.

       This liturgy recalls that
Lazarus was raised from the dead
by his friend, Jesus. The church
glorifies Christ as the Resurrection and the Life, who, by raising
Lazarus, has confirmed the resurrection of mankind. On this
icon, Christ's two-fingered blessing clearly forms the *IC XC*
(Greek abbreviation for Jesus
Christ), with the small finger
projecting to indicate the *I.* An
unusual feature of this icon, as in
the PRESENTATION AT THE TEMPLE,
is the lack of inscription. The
holes in the back plate indicate
that the icon once was attached
to a backing of some sort. *VBE*

17 CHRIST, MEDALLION OF
  DJOUMATI
  Gold, cloisonné enamel
  12th century
  3 x 3 in. (7.5 x 7.5 cm.)
  (top)

This medallion decorated the icon of the archangel Michael of the monastery of Djoumati in Gouria. Christ is shown offering the traditional benediction with his right hand; in the left he holds the gospel. The name Jesus Christ is inscribed in Old Georgian on the face of the medallion. This icon was part of the Botkin collection and was returned to Georgia in 1923. *TPS*

18 ST. DEMETRIUS,
  MEDALLION OF DJOUMATI
  Gold, cloisonné enamel
  12th century
  3 x 3 in. (7.5 x 7.5 cm.)
  (bottom)

This medallion, which because of the stylistic similarity is thought to have been made by the same artist who created the Christ medallion, was also used to decorate the icon of the archangel Michael of the monastery of Djoumati. The inscription in Old Georgian gives the name St. Demetrius. This piece was also part of the Botkin collection. In addition to the Djoumati monastery medallions in the State Art Museum of Georgia, there are related medallions from the Djoumati monastery in collections in Kiev and Madrid. The icons to which they were affixed, however, have been lost. *TPS*

19 ST. GEORGE
    Gold, cloisonné enamel
    15th century
    6¾ x 4⅞ in. (17 x 12.5 cm.)

In contrast to the uniquely Georgian theme of St. George slaying the emperor Diocletian, this rendering—St. George on horseback killing the dragon and rescuing a princess—is a popular scene common to Eastern Orthodox icons. The book of Revelation describes the dragon as the serpent of ancient days, who is a symbol of Satan, the Devil. The hand of Christ blessing from heaven can be seen in the upper right corner of the icon. The colors are bright, strongly contrasting with the gold background and the stark white steed. The Greek letters spell *Oagios Georgios* (Saint George), which is also spelled out in Old Georgian uncials. Holes through the metal indicate that the icon was once attached to another object, perhaps a wood support. *VBE*

Out of respect for the Greek Orthodox Church, it was often customary to include inscriptions in Greek as well as Old Georgian. This icon is a particularly late example of Georgian cloisonné enamel. The technique of cloisonné was lost to Georgian craftsmen during the late feudal era, a period in which Georgia suffered from a series of devastating invasions. *TPS*

20　John the Baptist,
　　 Icon of Telavi
　　 Gilded silver
　　 Late 16th century
　　 13 x 9¼ x ¾ in.
　　 (33 x 23.5 x 2 cm.)

The raised hand of St. John the Baptist demonstrates the traditional Eastern Orthodox form of bestowing a benediction by forming the Greek abbreviation for the name of Jesus Christ, *IC XC*, with the fingers of the right hand.

　　 According to the Gospel of Mark, John was the fulfillment of the prophecy of Isaiah. John began to baptize men in the desert, proclaiming baptism as a change of heart and the forgiveness of sin. People came to the river Jordan to be baptized and to publicly confess their sins. John preached that "There is someone coming after me who is stronger than I—indeed I am not good enough to kneel down and undo his shoes. I have baptized you with water, but he will baptize you with the Holy Spirit." Soon after, Jesus came from the Galilean village of Nazareth and was baptized by John in the river Jordan.

　　 The Gospel of Mark also states that John was dressed in camel's hair, with a leather belt. This type of clothing was a sign of penance and humility, for the desert was hot and the clothing scratched the skin. In this icon John is portrayed as an ascetic with unkempt long hair, untrimmed beard, coarse clothing, and bare feet. The scroll has a Gospel text in Old Georgian. Inscriptions near St. John's halo identify him, and inscriptions at the base of the icon state that it was offered to the church of Telavi by Edicher Tcholokachvili. St. John is variously called the Forerunner, the Baptizer, and the Precursor. *VBE*

21 THE VIRGIN,
    ICON OF BITCHVINTA
    Gold, silver, turquoises,
    sapphires, rubies
    1588
    15½ x 12¾ in. (39.5 x 32.5 cm.)

This icon, which also served as a reliquary, shows the Mother of God in the standing Hodigitria pose with the Child Immanuel. The influence of the Near East is apparent in the profusion of ornament, including precious stones and a highly decorated surface that incorporates the traditional grape leaf and floral motif. Archangels Gabriel and Michael appear in the upper right and left of the icon, and two sainted priests appear in the lower half.

There are inscriptions in Old Georgian along the border. An inscription on the reverse notes the exact date (1588) and the name of the donor, Mamia Dadiani, ruler of Samegrelo, who offered the icon to the church of Bitchvinta. *TPS*

22 ICON OF THE VIRGIN AND
    CHILD OF AKHALI-SHOUAMTA
    Gold, gilded silver,
    turquoises, pearls,
    semiprecious stones
    16th century
    19¼ x 16⅜ x 1¼ in.
    (49 x 41.5 x 3 cm.)

In the sixteenth century there
were two schools of metalwork
in Georgia. The work of the eastern school, reflecting the influence of the Near East and especially Persia, is characterized by
an emphasis on intricate surface
design and an abundant use of
semiprecious stones. In contrast,
the icons of the western school
remain simple in form and
decoration. This icon is from the
monastery of Akhali-Shouamta
in the eastern part of Georgia. *TPS*

The faces are painted on
wood and the metal has been
removed to expose the faces and
necks of the Mother of God and
Christ Child. In this Hodigitria
iconography, Mary is portrayed
to the waist, and the entire figure
of the child Jesus sits facing for-
ward in the crook of her left arm,
as in the standing poses. Donor
inscriptions on the reverse refer
to King Levan and his wife,
Queen Tinatine. Minute inscriptions in Greek have been chased
into the garments on the front of
the icon. *VBE*

23 TRIPTYCH OF ALAVERDI
Silver, gilded silver,
semiprecious stones
16th century
23⅝ x 13⅝ in. (60 x 34.5 cm.)

Christ Pantocrator and two
angels fill the upper arch of the
central panel. The right hand of
Jesus is shown in a traditional
blessing. The archangel Gabriel
appears in the upper left arch,
the Mother of God in the upper
right arch. Together they form
the composition of the Annunciation in which God's messenger,
the archangel Gabriel, announces
to the young Mary that she is to
become the Mother of God. Two
registers of three figures each
on either wing depict the twelve
apostles. The background of the
entire triptych is worked in a
floral pattern. The Old Georgian
inscriptions below the removable
central icon describe the donation
of the icon to the church of the
Mother of God of Kvarelia. *VBE*

24 THE SAVIOUR,
    ICON OF NESPERI
    Gilded silver, turquoises,
    carnelians
    16th century
    12⅝ x 8⅝ x ¾ in.
    (32 x 22 x 2 cm.)

Christ is shown in his tomb,
from the waist up—a compara-
tively rare depiction. Around the
head of Christ are turquoises and
carnelians. The background is
decorated with a traditional
Georgian motif of grape leaves
and flowers. The icon bears an
Old Georgian inscription with
the name of Maxim, archbishop
of Tsaïcha, who donated the icon
to the church of the village of
Tchala. *TPS*

25   GOLD BREAST CROSS
    Gold, rubies, pearls,
    enamel
    17th century
    11⅞ in.; cross 3⅛ in.
    (30 cm.; cross 8 cm.)

This seventeenth-century breast
cross features typical Eastern
Orthodox bulbous trefoil forms
on each of the four arms. *VBE*

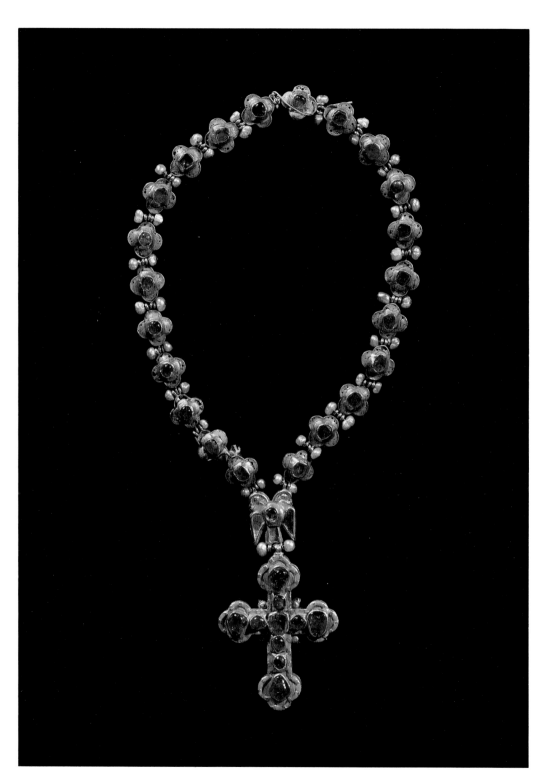

26 BIRTH OF CHRIST,
    ICON OF KATSKHI
    Gilded silver, pearls, tur-
    quoises, ruby-colored stones
    17th century
    10¼ x 6¾ in. (26 x 17 cm.)

This traditional Georgian icon was made by repoussé and chasing. The icon tells the story of the Nativity, or birth of Christ. Two angels flank the half figure of the Mother of God, whose halo is decorated with pearls, turquoises, and ruby-colored stones. Four angels in the heavens announce the birth of the Christ Child. Animals in the manger watch over the infant, who is swaddled in cloth, as was the custom for newborns. The star of Bethlehem, shining in the sky, guides the three kings bearing gifts to the baby Jesus. Three shepherds keep watch over their sheep. A second and smaller image of the Mother of God, dressed in flowing robes and shown in a reclining position, appears within its own outline on the lower right. In the center of the lower portion, two women are shown preparing to bathe the infant. Joseph sits dejectedly in the lower right corner. Some

Orthodox icons of the Nativity explain the dejection of Joseph by showing him tempted by a man (the Devil) with evil thoughts about his wife, who was betrothed to him after she conceived Jesus and yet "knew not man." *VBE*

The icon bears an inscription mentioning the donor, David Abachidze, and his wife, Nestan-Daredjan. The icon was offered to the monastery of Katskhi in the first half of the seventeenth century. *TPS*

27 DIADEM
Gold, semiprecious stones,
pearls
18th century
8¼ x 1¾ in. (21 x 4.5 cm.)

This eighteenth-century diadem
is decorated with semiprecious
stones and pearls. Gold flowers
inset with stones and pearls form
the upper row. *TPS*

The diadem and pendant
(fig. 28) are interesting examples
of Tbilisi workmanship with
Oriental or Persian overtones.
Holes in each end of the diadem
indicate that it once had other
components. *VBE*

28 PENDANT
Gold, painted enamel,
diamonds, emeralds, rubies
18th century
3½ x 2 in. (9 x 5 cm.)

The pendant has a section of
painted enamel in a red and blue
floral design on a white base.
Painted enamel was popular in
the production of Georgian
jewelry after the technique of
cloisonné was lost to Georgian
artists in the fifteenth century.
TPS

29 BREAST CROSS
Gold, painted enamel,
diamonds, emeralds, rubies,
pearls
18th century
11 x 3⅛ in. (28 x 8 cm.)

This piece is typical of the breast
crosses worn by Georgian bishops
in the eighteenth century. The
cross is decorated with many
precious stones and pearls, the
latter being especially favored by
Georgians. The cross and the
two-headed eagle above it are
made of painted enamel. *TPS*

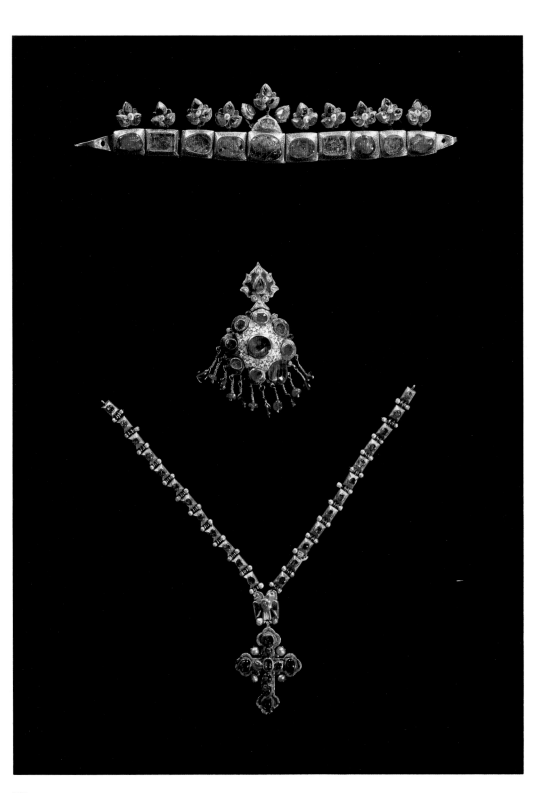

30 ST. GEORGE,
    ICON OF ZOUGDIDI
    Papou Meounargia
    Gilded silver
    1849
    12 x 9⅞ in. (30.5 x 25 cm.)

This icon is a very popular representation, that of St. George slaying a dragon. Legend has it that the well of a small village was inhabited by a dragon. The dragon would trade one jar of water for a beautiful girl, who subsequently became a meal for the beast. When it was the princess's turn to be traded, she cried out in fear, which raised St. George from the dead. Coming from the sky, he killed the dragon—the symbol of evil—and saved the princess. St. George never looks at the dragon because he does not want to see evil.

This tale and its representations suggest the triumph of kindness over evil. Another depiction, St. George slaying the emperor Diocletian, can be interpreted as the symbolic triumph of Christianity over paganism.

The inscription on the central portion of the icon and on the frame mentions Papou Meounargia, a famous Georgian silversmith, and the donors, David Dadiani, ruler of Megrelia, and Catherine, his wife. Papou Meounargia was a self-taught artist and one of the last of the nineteenth-century Georgian craftsmen to utilize traditional techniques of repoussé and chasing. *TPS*